Spirit, Hurry

poems by
Rolly Kent

Confluence Press 1985
A James R. Hepworth Book

*Some of the poems in this book first appeared in
the following periodicals and anthologies:* The Ardis
Anthology of New American Poetry; Coyote; Ironwood;
Mazagine; Seneca Review; Sonora Review; Threepenny Review.

A James R. Hepworth Book

Cover painting: *Dream 2* by Margo Burwell

Designed by Margo Burwell.

*Published by Confluence Press
at Lewis-Clark State College,
Lewiston, Idaho 83501*

Printed in the United States of America.

Library of Congress Catalog Card Number 85-070799

Distributed to the trade by Kampmann & Company, Inc.,
9 East 40 Street, New York, New York 10016

ISBN 0-917652-50-9 (paper)
ISBN 0-917652-51-7 (cloth)

TABLE OF CONTENTS

All that a man has to say or do that can possibly concern mankind, is in some shape or other to tell the story of his love— to sing; and, if he is fortunate and keeps alive, he will be forever in love. This alone is to be alive to the extremities.

—Thoreau, Journals

"And," said the lady, "if you should lose each other as you go through the— the— I never can remember the name of that country,— do not be afraid, but go on and on."

—George McDonald, The Golden Key

Is there a small country, some small
perfect country whose people love life so much
they never go anywhere else, though the rivers
flow from emerald to azure and pretty boats sail?
Is there a kingdom, a duchy, a county
where the roads are kempt with hedge and flower
and no one travels in or out?
Isn't there one country where people have
respect for death and therefore work to make
fifty or a hundred times more awareness
than now exists? I think there is such a country
because I remember those people loved good food
and clean clothes, I can tell you they lived
without one temple or university,
without a monument or shrine, a country
with nothing to build and nothing to finish
except the reckoning of happiness, and for that
they leave short ropes out in the open;
when a child ties the ends together he is ready
to grow up. A day's big event? —A rooster crowing;
in the next town over, dogs weep for the moon.
Such a place is not found in map or text
and yet has anyone failed to see the travelers,
the refugees on their way?
Human beings! We want everything, we settle for hope,
and mostly we just want something to happen,
and somewhere it *is* happening, friend,
to you and me— we are beginning again
with footsteps and rain, with other seasons
and a beautiful, new person, and when the sun comes around
we can't resist believing time is only
the long shadow of small, worn-out mountains.

PART OF THE NIGHT IN FLORIDA

I was only a child in a fat man's lap,
a boy merging with cigar smoke and stories
that all began: *One time in Michigan.* . .
I would doze and wake to Uncle Pete's big laugh.
I thought it was all part of the night in Florida.
I had forgotten winter and I didn't even
notice the heap of wood. The quiet
became different when Pete stood up,
he sat me in a striped canvas chair
where I could watch the whole thing—
all the adults built the bonfire
until it swelled bigger than the house
with fruit crates and chairs and doors.
They piled on hay and magazines, suitcases
stuffed with clothes, someone tossed in
a uniform then a mattress and a bedstead,
even live branches with wigs of moss
and enormous pinecones the size of a boy's head,
and many boxes of letters and postcards
and finally all the men threw in their shirts,
the gasoline splashed and everyone stepped back.
Uncle Pete raised his glass of bourbon, looked at
every one of us there, flipped his cigar—
and I beheld with eyes bigger than diamonds
the fuel rear up and howl its roar of freedom,
from every cell of wood air rushed, the fire
ate itself and grew! That's when I heard the dove—
she was burning inside a shoebox! A bad mistake,
an awful joke! But Uncle Pete told me
she was really somewhere else,
I listened to try to hear where. . . She cooed softly
on and on into the flames, calm and lovely, the fire burned
and she sang and I slept and forgot it.
Now, lying in your arms I hear this same dove
outside our window, her voice is sweet
and steady, the same voice, the same dove
singing for nothing in her pure, animal eternity.

A HISTORY OF THE HEART IN SPRING

In the sweet mornings of the young spring
I take out the dog and say, *Go pee*
and the dog does my bidding. First with
my eyes, then my body I wander
through the garden, fondling the tips
of iceplants where gold and magenta
dazzles whirr. I poke around
as the first people did, they were more
gentle than is recognized. Here I scratch
among the rosemary, there pluck the pain
from the dying fig. The old black heart of man
has shrivelled, a dried knot of fruit, and
I am innocent again, I am better, I will
kiss instead of gobble— Look! The first
rosebud of the year! What was I
thinking a little while ago? It was
like this waxy red which tinctures my hand
with sadness. Strange bud, you cling to the bush
but spurn the leaves' logic. You'll bleed once,
and, like everything else that changes, open
your mouth and bloom. I look in my lap
at the pile of weeds, I heft them:
There again! That pang that rouges up my arms—
holding such limpness I feel a little lost,
could I be tending the poor animal
in the road? I remember now: All night someone
like me was dumping things into the big river
that runs out to earth and dawn.
In his sack were the shucked hearts
of angels. He meant no harm. Why should he
know what's downstream? These green hearts
on the bough hint how morning's joy must one day
hurt. I drop the weeds over the wall, and here's
the dog, smirking with dirt, she plops
the bone in her mouth at my feet. Come on,
dog, it's another day.

NEVADA FALLS

The sun low over mountains, I awoke
to water rushing by. My feet were wet
but my clothes had dried. The water's
one voice became many: two men lisping
kindnesses on each other's tweeds;
children tittering where lovers necked;
drunken laughter by the river's edge.

It was then, stretching the sleep
out of my arms, I reached into the cedar
above my head, and there saw it,
caught on a branch: a strand of golden hair.
I wound and unwound it through my fingers.
Then I took it from the tree. Something
swifter than a story happened
and passed, I felt a grief
huger than the mountains. My hands
began to burn. Birds took the distance home.
The air above green woods
wore a gown of sparks. There was a wide plain,
horses, a figure in a tower— I went
many times to that place, and the air
above those trees.

When I came back, the river was inside me.
I sat there in the twilight like a crazed
flower, closing out the cold.
Waiting for her my life began— young Tristan,
open-eyed and lost in a wilderness of love.

Everyone knows that tall trees tend to be
excessive in their intensity, and the date
palm is certainly no exception. Just a moment ago
I had this feeling, staring straight up a bald trunk
into the sparkling green fire, that I almost
understood. . . what— palm trees? blue?
—something I couldn't quite hold on to.
                                        The verge again!
How suddenly it comes! And how long and strange
the wait in ignorance till now, now once more,
about to know the merging of world and witness
into one vast emotion, poised—
                                        and
passed! Back to traffic, bells, old men
scrounging smokes, the patch of shade drifted;
it's too warm in the sun. I stare dumbly
at my sandals, a snail shell, tree, my face lifted
or lowered by what I think I see.
                                        Why don't
such instants endure? Or, why should they? And
what do *you* care anyhow? You are not here,
and these tall palms are hard to see even sitting
beneath them. Perhaps it was inconvenient
for you to come just now— I'm not complaining.
This green space is pretty and quiet, and it is good
to study oneself or simply sit and smoke; but
I wish you were with me. That is one reason
I like to make poems, just as, because of
circumstance, I must make up you. For your part,
do not feel remorse that I am here only in
your image of me. For at least in this way
it is possible to meditate together, even though
we are strangers who otherwise would not.
                                        Are we
so different? In the poem we are not. Here
it is easier, let this gorgeous, dark-haired
woman smiling walk by— the palm tree is
occupied with half the sky, I am but a man,
an atom of perfume left behind while the goddess

ambles from conducive sap away! Oh life out
of sight! You bequeath us sticky trees and increase—
we reach, but do we make you real?
                                                   End of afternoon,
near, perhaps, an ocean. Cars sough dully,
rustle and lift; the sea flaps those watery
wings of noise— shells, seeds ground
and softened in tides!
                         And slowly, as if
this great breath of sea interrupts nothing but
its own emergence, blue clouds begin
to wander, forming sky around us—
first sea, then a sky— overwhelming the resolve
of *this* and *this* and *this* with an inward event
that slips like a wave and crashes.
Soft ice-cream, a girl in tight shirt,
the arcades of pleasure anchor us again
in yearning. . . I'd settle for
a chew of taffy and let it go at that,
but this comic genius of palms dangles its cargo
of dates like mocking jesters' balls.
                                          Where do
emotions come from? How can they swing so suddenly
from the tree of life like a pack of
filthy monkeys? I say, *the tall date palm*
and the date palm scorns me, stealing my attention
like the toy banana it is— Hey! Bring that back!
You may not have it! I only said there are five
big palms, five big poems in the vernacular
you and I are citizens of. The trees
don't answer. They are simply trees,
and I am only moving around in the silence
like palm trees swaying in space, exciting
some commotion by which you will know
I am here.
                 Do you think like this; does it
help; what do you cherish? Oh friction
can make us sparkle, friend, from conflict
let's grow wise! Although my own

8

daughter doubts it, hates it, yells, "You stupid
big fat grump!" and my wife goes alone
to the movies. Then I shuffle around, guilty,
bad, needing to start over.
                 Today
I thought of the gentle palms. "So nice!"
I scolded, "but you are not! Go,
unruly man, and learn civility!"
With lowered eyes I left my fellows,
scuffing among cats and cans,
shunning the thoroughfare, exposing my head
to the sun, suffering in perspiration my own offense;
until near the park I forgave myself.
                 And that
is how I happened to sit down in shit. And had to
get up and wipe my hand on some grass
and then on some paper and I was angry all over
again, but then how can you blame the birds?
Around the trunks of these tall trees
they have shit for years, and the hot lime has etched
the grass the way the Atlantic munched away my youth.
The date seeds the birdies couldn't manage
settle like gravel in snow, slowly sinking
toward earth's great maw.
               I remember something now,
from many years ago: I stepped in just
such a mass of what I thought at first were
candle droppings— not so white as these,
so fresh, but having a brown and stuccoed patina,
like mud-castles unshaped by rain. Onto the sidewalk
it had dripped from a wall. . . I stopped,
and my inner tumult stopped.
               I didn't know
what it was. I crouched down—
                 the street
was empty, and I was coming home
from Jeannie Rybicki's house on White Meadow Avenue.
It was always autumn when I came back empty-hearted
from her house. Along the street late afternoon

lay fetid, imposing a life-sentence
of loneliness in which I stared, age 15,
at this incongruity, this hive or ruins
of the future. Jeannie oh Jeannie
loved a guy named Norman, I knew him, that son of
Proteen Powder, grunting Bicep, Tricep
and Deltoid even unto Pectoral, Curley and Moe. Agh!
The sky was a slum, my home full of the cookies
of consolation and just-don't-help-her-have-a-baby.
How long I commiserated with this mystic goop
I don't recall, only that it finally called me
from the wallow I was in, and after awhile
I climbed out, undigested, and made one of those
odd gestures love sometimes demands:
                                    I sunk
my fingers slowly in the soft silt of bird-dirt;
my hand vanished; and still I did not stop,
but, seized with a new pleasure, plunged
the left hand in, lost in cool ooze. . . and then
a few cars passed and one honked
and the streetlights came on
and I did not know what it meant
but got up and went my way
without thinking about it.

SERVING GRAPES

Before anyone else, there were perfect
blue grapes. Before the sun: these grapes
under big sugary stars by the sea; and I
carried them like a lantern, a lock-box
of the unguent this passionate planet needs.
Once they were biped creatures named
Paco, Lorenzo, Galena and so forth,
geographers of the breast intoxicant.
They were moons. They were eyes by the road.
Horses near the mesa at night. Bubbles
that held briefly drowned passengers' cries.
Clocks, tribes, prayer flags, cairns; my mother's
birthday in May; the atmospheres of numbers;
the cripple's dream of her hands. Now in my hand
they are a rosary of questions about what
will become of the bodied, the absenting
from bodies; the ripening, the passing,
the shimmer, the drouth; this blue sky that
darkens our disappearance. Brothers, sisters,
I brought them to you from my trip away.
In memory I shall always be this one,
bearing them in a yellow dish toward you.

CLEANING UP TRASH AT 7 A.M.

I kick their chicken carcass
for the third time this week, and the big
carbolic bubble of Coke makes the same
bully sound the dodge-ball made
when it slapped the new kid's face.
Bounding down the driveway it hits
their house with goddammit and my dog
nipping after. Meanwhile someone
has been watching— upstairs a curtain
springs like a branch. . . the back door
slams, here comes the youngest daughter
harvesting mess into her pink nightie.
She rights the cans and frantically
starts to fill them, smiles at me, sorry.
She's very pretty, and pregnant.
And sorry, really sorry about the garbage,
it must be those dogs again, or a car. . .
She is more than pretty, almost avoids it,
pecking at scraps and bottle-tops—
she is so exquisite, in fact, I realize
how we know nothing at all
until such a face beholds us! By now
I am raking up tin-foil with my fingers,
but Mama at the window turns apoplectic
with the girl's name. Guess I have to go,
she says and hurries away,
leaving me under the old woman's one
living eye. Again the door slams;
the screaming starts, with short
gasps of silence where the blows must come;
and I walk carefully past their house,
following the dog into the soft
early light, amazed by the power of beauty.

January, the desert left to mull in wine
and raisins, mature month of my dog

earning her personhood: She pities
instead of chases cousin rabbit, she

remembers this is herself on the path
of purpose walking. My dog is a human being,

she is ready for the concrete bunker
where explosives for the quarry used to cool,

where now the transient quarter
in a cave of flasks and porn.

My dog looks, goes on; I look, go on,
forgetting the rug dragged into the valley

where some day soon my dog will doubtless
pass right by the twiggy legs of a dead man

in the brittlebush, the sunflower
of a hundred eyes and a hundred lamentations

that no one, not even my dog, can listen to.

CERTAIN STARS

We are sliding down deserted slopes
of the dark resort, the snow tonight the color
of dimmest stars, no moon here. Everyone grown
is a child again, a milk tooth jarred from gum,
a bit of crystal patience no one knows
what to do with after the last slide down.
If I spoke my heart and mind to a person
it would come out cracked and slurred, a shriek
or howl of laughter, so I say nothing, and
one by one my friends look at me
then go on sledding, parkas of smudge on snow.

I know there are certain stars, unseen peewee ones,
that burn not for love of themselves, as do I,
but for God before the word shone— I wonder
you aren't brighter, stars, what keeps you dim?
Are you done, your fierce act burned
from outside in and now you wait? Stars,
were you ever scared, did you ever cry out,
Stop! I refuse! when you learned you
belong not to yourselves but to burning?
And the longer you worked to outlast it
the wilder the flames grew, the cinder
yawning in the middle. . .

I want to say something like a star feels
when I stand under you, asking for a comfort.
But I wonder, stars, I really wonder
if it helps to know: Stolen or gladly given back,
God takes it all, everything is on fire
and that is why I see, though more dimly
than even one of you, stars, even one dim star
that might see me on the quiet hill.

Sometimes the hill on Bella Vista
seems to ascend not geography but
time, and it is going to take me lives
to return to my backdoor, the woman
in the kitchen will scream
at my antique face. . .

As always I walk the hill like a pantomime,
toe heel, toe heel,
a little behind my thoughts, watching
the heavens for the end of the stairs.
Two nights ago I saw
a green horsetail swish across the mountains,
the greenness of that fire made me gasp!
I would like to believe it fell inside me
for two entire days and any minute
a voice will say, Rolly!
Rolly Rolly Rolly! Arise
with your loves and go
to southern France!

No, my teeth clatter that. Tonight
this cold is a veneration of all the breaths
I have breathed into disappearance, breathed
and forgot, breathed and forgot, who
would bother to remember each? Yet if I
could, if I could track just one
beyond the houses dark with common sense,
I know I'd cross at last the customs hut
fraying at the end of protocol's thought.

Oh distant hour when we are neither
man nor mother!— At the window
a figure glows in a cloud of steam

on the cold, cold pane, a person
rubbing away what can be seen,
the better to precinct the dark.

Into that glow I'll pass, shadow
whose reverie this clandestine life has been.
Spirit of that time, speed onward in your phaeton
through the suburbs of stars. Tonight
I am breathing on the window for you.

Ah, here's the morning! I punch off
the radio, slide from bed— my first
step lands on the dog asleep, and
of course the second goes through the hole
in my pants, enlarging
the Bardo of Entanglement in the Tear,
the terrible Buddha of my knee grinning
as I shovel into sneakers and damnitall!
But soft you awhile! What a·bed have we here,
ol' sleepyhead that loves not
the work of the world? I bend to kiss those ruby
lips but bite her nose instead, run into
the kitchen. "That was mean, you crud,"
she moans. "Take out the dog."
                                    Life,
you are my faithful companion, but the dog
needs a poke to get going, or,
alternatively, love. I ruffle her muzzle
and we salute the serious back door. These keys
are cool and dreamy, the action of the lock
satisfies my innermost needs!
                                    Outside:
astringent air, and the east yawning yellow —
                                                Sunday!
How cold and quiet. No one else! Standing
on my wall like this I feel smug, but I won't
hoot or howl, just frisk my ribs. Hunh—
there goes the moon behind the roof,
off to a tryst in its canoe. . . And now,
                                    Ladies
and Gentlemen! Introducing. . .
my reason for living. . .
a yardful of
Bermuda!
        Just looking at it makes me sweat.
I get down on hands and knees
and yank up grass, for it has
grown two feet high and shameless. Even pulled
Bermuda will rise again like the avatar

of time to cover my cactus with twilight.
So I dig, first with a trowel,
then my hands, into the web of work.
                                    Sweat
mists my arms and chest. The sun
climbs: I inch down brittle bannisters of root,
blinded by salt and dog-slobber,
nails bursting with dirt. There's no humoring
this hard-pan! Just claw at it,
the big, senseless syllables of breath
roll like breakers over the tongue
                                    but
                                        the root
snaps anyhow,
grass of a month of Sundays.
                            I powder the dirt
on my fingers and drift. I hate weeding. I want to
sit in this dried-out bed of earthweed
lifting handfuls of dirt like a moron,
35 going on 4, my father repeating, "For the last time,
come along, boy, for your constitution!" I just
want to sift the ocean sand while
the breeze sifts me! But for the last time, again,
he convinces me to help the crabs, "That's our job—
walk every morning and help those crabbies
grind the sand! Why look what they did
last night alone. They must be tired, too."
I go to my work gladly, the sea sips my feet,
sighs, so happy! And I am, too, to do what I can.
I whisper thanks into six crabholes,
                            and 30 years later
on breath we come, on breath depart: Gulf Coast or
Jersey shore, Midwest or Arizona, it's
the same immortal meal set before us, a world
that is the ardent wooer's task!
                            Yes, today's
the day I shovel the rubble at last! I'll
bundle the scraps of 2 x 4, pluck up
fossil turds, thistles, trash,

prune the trees and hedges. I'll claim this
sloppy yard in the name of human decency! But first
I'll rest.
    Oh perhaps I am
a shameless, lazy man, my small heart
doomed to ring only in the cathedral of intentions:
one. . .
        two. . .
            echoes of seven o'clock
die. . . suddenly
fly up in so many cries and white wings! Ha!
These things of rain and sun! So numerous
and impossible to number— morning
crying out for more! More
dog turds and dirt! More sunlight! Bermuda!
Continents! Men!
More rising up and falling back, more
arising again!
        From the door, the righteous halloo!
From this mess, a firmament of eggs
scrambled in salsa! Oranges quartered! Cafe au lait!
Bisquits! Bacon! Ear bent up, "Up!
Get up and wash those hands!" And I go, I'll go!
I splash around singing *Gloria!*
G-L-O-R-I-A Gloria! steering the sink nowhere,
losing the soap, losing the verse, falling
silent as Noah did when his dove, too,
was lost and he heard the waters say, *Once. . .*
and he understood and taught it to the world,
back in the days when nothing could tame us.

MONUMENTAL TOPLESS DANCER

(photo by Diane Arbus)

The disposition of her breasts may seem all,
even to Leonardo in the corner, the shoe salesman,
the photographer, the geek: Civilization
bulges from epicenters of big gestures, yet
with nonchalance of one bored finger
she dimples a breast. . . silicon or icon,
she's America's mama, the saint behind Uncle Sam,
it's our gig, boys, to bury our faces
and feed!
The Master said,
I am the madonna your thinking turns to wax
then spangles with fruit and song bird. You
shall be candles, be salts, be consumed in loaves.
But the next time, He didn't speak at all;
He became a monumental topless dancer
and our hands pulled into the driveway
and opened the girl's blouse. Oh childhood paraboli,
oh largesse of what might be, disguised as
sunny doves, cups of sugar, roses, snow or,
back from the war, pure kid gloves!
                              OK, forget
the photo. Forget the genius of His move:
                                        Sated
on sea-swells, Cristóbal Colón surveyed
the night, then wrote: *The torment is like a fever.*
He saw a woman hover upon the storm, part it,
the surcease offer him at his watch. Capitán
let the chapbook fall, and in palimpsests of air
discovered breasts so generous and apt,
so glamorous, he whimpered and wept for his apposition.
How many times Columbus must caress! For try as he did
with eyes or hands or lips, he never could remember
what it was, nor what, exactly, he was doing—
would you, brothers? All night the spirit visited,
she even wished him in Italian to have
the world he wanted; but all that great man could do
was call her Columbia and sail on, confident, to India.

(Hopi wafer bread made from blue corn meal)

The bread which Rachel serves me
is the corn's blue sky. Even
touch such manna: All over
my hands and clothes the blue
scroll flakes and blows!

What's it mean, piki? What's
inside— an antedeluvian encyclical?
Masau's migratory chart? Revelations
from Pharaoh's priests? The emptiness
Big Mind thinks in? Or Mr. Bug's
mindless nothing, boring the corn?

I'll tell you what I know: It's
a fine April day. All the blue
moths of the mesa are flying.
Each spring, back and forth they go,
pets of the sun. I watched
the little boy outside snare one
and roll up his shy feelings
within those piki-ish wings. I saw
him spit on his treasure and
hold it shut, whirl it at the end
of his arm through the air, dry,
then come around to the back door,
knock and run away! Yes, I watched
all this progress, this
sacred little note, delivered
up the ladder from winter
to spring, from boy to man, pupil
to pupil, this love note,
this love note from Rachel,
right here in my hands!

As gentle as I am and patient,
as handsome and true, all
my good qualities not-
withstanding, as I simply
try to open it

and tease loose the esoteric
letters of love, the frailty
of formal matter and my two
clumsy mits make a mess
of text, map, the archaic
lamp of wings.

"What are you doing?" she says. "It's
bread, you just
eat it!"
I open my mouth; she puts
a wafer on my tongue. I hold it
there and wait: dissolves like
snow in the tomb of teeth, then, after
thought, a faint glyph of sweetness.

So, dear friends, I ate the bread
they call piki, the corn's
famous scroll. Inside
was a poem about piki, which Rachel
gave to me, smiling.

THE RAIN THAT DAY

for my sister

Having looked a long time, I listened to what
I could not see lengthen beyond the house,
leaving its smell in the screens. For half
a minute the hair on our arms stood still, then
thunder collapsed the sky like a vein of ore—
you jumped into the chair, and finding nothing
out the window, fell asleep against me.
Pest, just then the rain stopped; in its place
a crystal grew around the space for rain.
"Rain," I said. The air stung.
Where was the music the crystal hid?
When I looked from my window, sunlight
bubbled out of the wall. Into your cheek
garish, slip-cover hibiscus bloomed
softer, pink. I wished I were the one asleep.
The roiling gutter made me ache, the steam
on the street, dew. That day I didn't
pinch or bite you, yet, but, halting like rain
between one then and another— I saw you. . .
then jerked your arm. "It's over.
Let's go outside." We walked behind the dog-coop
where honeysuckle grew and I sent you in
to pick them, looked around— and
shook the branches till you nearly drowned.
Mom yelled from the kitchen,
"Leave your sister alone!"
How could I resist? I let you chew the petals
and hawk out bitter pap. "No," I said, "like this:"
You raised a little yellow trumpet
to your lips, murmured *mmmm* and drew in the songs
that since have made you weep without knowing why.

NEW MOON

Since sundown I've been sitting on the steps
drinking a beer, watching the new moon
descend toward mountains. The smell
of alfalfa makes me close my eyes— the valley
broadens all at once, as if I could see
through to another side
where remembrance extends us forever. . .
When I open my eyes the air glows for 50 miles
in this spray of light. The Nopah Range
gleams like smoky agate, becoming
pure shadow, deep and fathomless. A man could
reach in and not want to
come back, ever. Out of blue water, slowly
coming down, the net of stars falls,
drawing the moon to shore, and I am suddenly
in the middle of all this beauty, crying.
The mountains reach for the moon, the moon
almost touches them—

I am like that, a memory
pulled to a certain shape on earth. The heart
circulates the moon through the body, but what
engine of separation is driving everything farther
onto the mystery, leaving in its wake
this person I know? The moon is a feeling
that will always sail back to the horizon of
what's been left; and yet, on board is a shadow
older than ships, vague as the face
that jumped to sea: cold, worn thin like
a widow's ring, like the human past, becoming
featureless and smooth as a breast.

HANGING CLOTHES

Whenever the president of some country speaks,
when there are riots in Boston and Tokyo
and the hunger of whole continents
stares from the empty carton,
I get out the dirty laundry
and carry big baskets of wet clothes
down to the line.

I hang a little dress, a sunsuit, some pants.
I take my time with a nightgown, a blouse, some tights.
I pat the air in panties, let the bras and hankies
fill up like spinakers and when
the clothesline is fitted out
I sail around the dungarees to the Orient
for cinnamon and to the South for hides and coffee.
I bury my face in shirts and breathe
an ocean of chemise and scarf.
I travel through the pajamas
and trade underpants with the Islanders,
at Casablanca, contraband and smoked goat,
and in the Baltic I drink till my socks are dry.

Along the rivers and near the wharves,
in alleys and backyards,
through the late afternoon I think of the size
of this world, think of all its breasts
and crotches, its stained armpits
and strained or slender throats, think of
the muscle in sleeve and leg and the arches of feet,
I think of use, the whitegoods
shining with the shadow of trees.

The flies circle my head. Everything's
plain as sheets.
I take my time.
The towels and jeans
will be hard and sweet with sunlight.

FATHERS AND SONS

You asked them once what *he* was the hero of;
instead, Jesus raised some fish-sticks from the dead.
Some men are like that— women raise their sons
the way the moon brings up tides onto the intimate beach.
Expanses have always lured you; what son
doesn't long for the pure, invented other?
Call it freedom; call it *our father.* The planet
turns its horizons into the long ago.
                              There was this
war once. Your father entered the lonely streets
where the armies were piled, dyed in the inky wool
of heritage. He paused at a door
and told a joke; then he left. That was his style.
The women left in stitches and sewed the house shut.
So what is missing gets coated
with a voice, and even from beyond the pale
a father can jump into his son's years,
yank the ripcord— like that
he's here again! And,
                              can you believe it?— here
you are, plunging ahead deeper into a life so
familiar, you started to tell a story whose hero,
at least, could die of the difference.
                              Coronado,
Ponce de León— remember Cabeza de Vaca? After he
wrecked on Galveston Island and escaped his savage captors,
he ran into the day when strangers in the west
already knew he could free them from themselves:
He began to cure the sick, even revived a dead man.
People praised his path with flowers, women,
the hearts of 500 deer. What power they wished
on him! Yet in the end, he wanted only
to go home. Of course, that was long ago, and he's
gone, too, except for a story. That's the way it is
with gravity— the phone rings, earth and home

want us back, and we who inherit make up a voice
worth the cost of the call.   Every word *is* a call,
and a response. Look around if you don't believe it.
You can't lie on the cot between breaths for long
without noticing the others, your brothers, all of you
are dragging the sky by its ribbons down to where
fathers have gone. Whose hands will you look for now?
Through the ghetto of the genuine you poke the rubble.
You hang the doors, reglaze all the windows. This
is the world? Call it what you like, or just
explain it. It's yours.

WHAT THE STORM DID

After the stormy night, dark moons
sailed in the orange tree.
I was zipping my pants when I saw them.
"Look what the storm has done," I thought
and went out in my socks to be near them.

Cold globes of sleep, one for each hand.
Maybe I just closed my eyes.
Or stared into the hedge. The dirt.
The roof-tiles along the hill.
One by one the morning took its turns:

a man bare-chested on the corner,
looking straight up; two spiders
descending the woodpile; some frost in shadow
like a heart-shaped field of snow—
one by one, proceeding.

You called me from the kitchen then,
said my name like Fido and whistled twice.
Maybe my eyes were closed. There was no man
when I looked, no bird, spiders, heart,
no hard dark moons.

I took my hands into the kitchen
and warmed them on your eyes.
"Oooo," you said. "Guess who."
We sat at the table quietly,
eating your strange cakes and butter.

MY DEATH AND CLOUDS

The city won't miss a step
of its cowboy waltz, I certainly wouldn't,
not for my cortege.
The tired cop understands: Cloud-pure,
suited with sashes and bands, he hasn't
pledged his heart to dust and hankies,
though he salutes for the show:
My beautiful death is passing by,
and the radio fills with traffic
of clouds. Clouds building a city
exactly like this, its just citizens
just like me: Goofy,
Hot Head, Lady Luck, Fool. . .
by afternoon who isn't full of it?
The day I die. . .
These are the clouds.
The day I die. . .
This is what I wanted.
Rain splatters its homage across the ground
and the dust leaps up like little frogs. Upon what
did happiness rely, upon whom? The still
faces float by. Were they me? Am I I? The clouds
rise up to feast on no answer, to dance
over the grim and busy graves.

MESAS LIKE HATS

The sun is gathering bottles like a spry
old man, many thousands of amber eyes
toss and blink inside the empties. The moment
winks: Where the horizon is a plaza
men are dancing around some funny hats!
Such hats! They aren't fedoras or derbies
or caps or beanies or top-hats made
of beaver, not even gallons of Stetson
from Mrs. Earth's Haberdashers.
Here are the hats from the whirl-wind
the Milky Way was fashioned of.
                                        All this dust!
Men are doing the hat dance. Violent men,
spinning and jumping on hats, reeling around,
throwing them up and stomping them down,
spitting and peeing on hats— no, it's not
a pretty sight!— drawing back like bowstrings
to leap headfirst into the crown of chaos!
It's the famous Navajo Navy,
home from wonderful lands with many
wonderful hats, drunk as hell on shore-leave,
ruining the beautiful creations
of the finest craftsmen. Aw, why not!
Plenty left, hats and evenings, to restore us
from the wreckage.
                        But just when the dance
is over, it isn't— out of nowhere
the final sailor comes, hikes his breeches,
and all the ladies stroll the port,
calling in the night. Something behind his back. . .
He saunters over. . . pulls out— flowers?
It's another hat! A perfectly black,
immaculate hat, and flings it high above
our heads. Whooo-weee! It rises and rises;
he leaps after— not one woman will catch him!
Whooo-ooo-weee! Whooooooo-weee! Everyone whirls
and falls down silly.
                        Overhead the sailor's boots
have set, twin moons brimming the deepening hat;

the rest of him is gone. The women get up
and wander, there's red dust on their lips,
it's in their hair. . . Jesus, I'm impressed,
I mean, I had no idea! They aren't, after all,
deer! Just ladies on their way to work,
faces glistening as they giggle
behind their hands. What a beautiful night!
And those sailors!
                    Just ordinary men
from the sea, left to themselves to sleep it off.
Already they have sailed into the night again,
and around the giddy girth of the globe
they slip their arms and sigh. Oh they'll be back!
With hats to amaze you, boots from the hooves
of delicate beasts!
                    Yes, friend, this world
abounds in wonders that never cease their
search for us to sing and dance and whoop!
But tomorrow, tomorrow. Let them go.
The boat of sleep is rocking and the sun
is gone, shh.
                    Goodnight, dear people, goodnight!
Thanks for the dance and the funny hats. I liked
how you ruined them, ruined them all, except
the perfect hat of the sky. Soon I'll tip it
over my face, too, and join you in sleep,
everything left behind but thanks, and these
ten thousand million stars
shaking in mid-air with laughter!

I WENT OUT THE DOOR

I went out the door screaming Fuck you
yelling it two more times before I
jumped the wall and headed up the road
scaring dogs with my wild tap-dance
snarling at the yellow winter dust
hating a stupid dogshit that looked like
a rock to kick hating the rock that fell
in the path where the goddamned thing
didn't belong split into three wisecracks
nine stupid jokes and hundreds of miniscule
mica glands
          not even a mile from home
and I'm lost lost in my pride too stupid
to say I'm sorry too stupid to get up go home
stop jabbing poking stabbing this white fungus
that is really not a fungus but
a bleached-out flipflop some girl
dropped with her panties and the shrine I
stared at from the road is up close
just another firepit for gypsies another
rabbit spit one more plastic gallon some Rosarita
beans .22 shells a whole case of beer
riddled like a gangland hit
              why do I
find these things this way
whacking through branches
it would have been spring again for the
wren's nest but someone chopped it from cholla
sap still oozes on the severed canes
inside the nest it is plush pink
insulation from the new houses by the river
80 trips up and back a mile each way
160 miles times two birds over 300 miles
ripping off the great
Downtown Redevelopment Corporation here is
our replica the paths from the door
the transits home again the tiny wanderers

weaving what is and is and is always this same
lopped uterus exhausted
inside three eggs buff
perfect we were taught never touch them
maybe the birds will return what will
help us now to what dim creature of caves or
decayed starlight can I bow down and say
I'm still a child
still a child

MY STAR

Tonight my favorite star is so low in the sky
this is the last time I'll find it there. Star,
when you return next year, what shape
will you assume? Light beckons us strange animals
to lift our heads and look. Another season
says goodbye, my star bows down to the ground.
So memory dies: grows, fills, falls, a plump
fruit of yellow light, ripening towards earth
and summer. Everything that lives becomes, *is*,
something that happened before. Whatever else

my star is now, it looks like Granny did
the night she wanted to run away, and would have,
except we brought her home. When her laughter
cracked my sleep that night, the yard was in
an iron trough only fireflies pierced.
Down in the drive Grandma sang about the glow-
worm glitter, but when her hands threshed
the air in tune, a galaxy of motes gathered
and pulsed around her. The song stopped; Grandma

opened her arms— the fireflies entered. "Here
comes the bride, short bald and wide!" over
and over she sang. The bugs in her mouth
made her giggle; she snatched up more to eat.
"Granny, don't!" I yelled, surprised by my voice,
and hers— "They're my stars! Not yours."
Our laughter rippled. The door banged—

I jumped into bed, waiting. Soon
on the stairs Grandma sobbed to be let go,
let go! "Stop it!" my mother hissed. "It's
too late to leave tonight. Tomorrow." After awhile
the whispering ceased; Granny snored; the house

sank into breath. I creeped from the canopy
of a pounding heart and hid beneath the window.

I thought stars were where the outcome starts,
above the litter of trees and planets. I looked;
it was only dark, and so still and empty
when God glanced back a moment
a fat spark shot from his mane; then He
went on, leaving us alone with our bodies.

LUCIANO

In hand the bird gets smaller and smaller,
its beaded eye a sunset caviar. In this way, the Will
slips through: egg shells, fingers, the asteroid belt—
sinking, ascending, it travels on, and the angels
gnash their teeth and hide— even angels
who by fistfuls pound this bird to dust and drop
the ballast over, even the angels know Luciano,
and they don't want him either.

Luciano lives in the hills above the ceiling,
roving in those spaces he used to rove so well.
In earlier epochs we slept much lighter
listening for his return. Now we are like articles
we adjusted to: books and sidewalks, exhaust pipes,
shoes. What were the bounds Luciano knew
beneath those tinted domes! He showed our passion
around the sky, those men and women flew! Though
like us plummeted. And like Luciano!

Luciano will not be that bird again, he cannot be
another bird except the one he is for us.
I have never seen his beak, but I've heard him
knock so loud the water trembled in my drinking glass.
He came to me when all I saw was ugliness and low
ceilings. I liberated joists, I hosed down
noxious insulation, I stooped and cast up pony walls,
plaster boards. I called for imperial finish
and fussed the color till it was right; and when my walls
and ceilings blushed in freshets, I forgot what the world is;
but all the while Luciano was there, even when I didn't know.

He had slipped among us like a spore with hooks,
and before he was anything at all, such as radio waves
or color, he lived in a stardust nest, a real innocent.
I would like to ask him what happened, and what, if anything,
he recalls. Luciano, how many lifetimes does it take

to travel to my ceiling joists? What was the ceremony
they sent you with; and what is the point of doing
this, Luciano who can't sit upon a shoulder
and yodel or hatch one feather or shit. Isn't there
anything you'd like? A silver water dish, a hole
chopped in the roof! He is something, Luciano is,
he certainly is something, hurting himself in the rafters,
pecking away, trying to break through! But

oh Luciano, you are made for the age of imported
8 penny nails, permangate, thick as a pesto of iron
and sawdust, collision. All you do, my friend,
is wince and veer and crash. All you do is
pick yourself up and do something else which
ends up being the same thing! If I tell
a gentle story or whistle a pathetique, it only
stirs him into frenzy. If I crack spice and seeds,
or love him, it doesn't have any effect. He hasn't

come to the same conclusions; he hasn't come here
to love love or believe beliefs. To what can
Luciano's work be compared? All I can tell you is
there's a bird in my attic finishing something
I don't understand. His heart is all he ever believed in
and therefore he must eat it by nibbles and squeaks.
What he loved most tastes most bitter. And even when
it grows quiet up there, I still won't know, I'll just
sit like this beneath my ceiling. I'll know better
than to speak, I won't be crying. Luciano,
remembering you I'll remember the opposite of food
isn't hunger but forgiveness, which must be
where you are, my teacher and friend, my Luciano,
resting at last from chaos.

AFTER TEARS

It takes 45 minutes to cook the fat
out of the sausage
45 minutes in which to sing along
with the simmering brats
searing the casings with beer
tightening the skins
like conga drums
                Ten minutes ago
I'm in the tub spilling tears
drowning in stupidity
I can barely remember for what
some voice ululating in the faucet
some face in the water breaking up appealing for help
who was that guy
not even ten minutes ago globules
oinking from his eyes his nose his ruddy pores
sobbing into the towel who
                I don't know I'm
dancing around some sausages
from the market on Sixth Street
slapping the weinies with the spatula
sniffing the aromas of oregano and pepper
a croupy child remembering mama and the vaporizor
Doc Hiler and his clambakes six
green lobsters looking up from the pot
the good doctor incising the shell popping
the lobster inside out *Here eat this chubby boy*
                It's
nearly nine o'clock no one's home
there's forgiveness in the quiet room
all you can hear are the tears spitting
in the pan happiness is
splitting its sides the singer
leans overs his dinner-to-be

and mutters *Gut das ist gut*
little sausages he towels them off
it is the first time man ever knew
there is a way to do things
there is an affinity everything
right up to its demise has for affection
it's the very first time
a fork made sense or a mouth that blade
of grass in the head oh a thousand years
from now and everafter the keening of slaughter
will be music in God's mind

ADDING ON

The entire month of June smolders
in the steam above the coffee then trembles
under brown waters where my face bloats.
An unbearable slag of weeks shimmers
on this heap of knocked-down walls and roof.
And above the new room's naked blocks
another day hunkers: Steve,
destroying angel of carpentry, plots rafters,
bearing walls, bird's beaks, doom—
              How many
mornings beneath the pillow have I dreaded
my mind's work? Yet here I am again, in love
with the flinch and whine of Skilsaw,
the slobber of sun on my face, shadow in the dirt
like a burst bag of astral blood. What
have I begun? And who can separate
the smell of sweat from wet concrete?
              Oh terrible
god of coffee! Your favors demand we jitter.
Steve wrestles his tool-belt to the ground, leaps—
Lord preserve me from eyes like that! Poor devil,
his wits have twisted like pretzels in the sun.
"Another hot bugger, hunh, Steve?"
"Brother, you ain't a-wuffin!" he says and takes
a mug of coffee, damning in the same breath
Euclid and all his sons: "This sucker's gonna be
crooked, no way that last rafter'll ever be plumb!"
Nor him! He's down in the dirt, seized by fits
of numbers, dragging off his funny lines
for today's safari with symmetry. I soothe my eyes
with known things: grout joints, window frames,
even the dancing honeycomb of sky which,
stared into too long, makes men
dream-up houses.
           When I look up again
from nailing, the sun has flown the ridgepole.
Miranda is calling from her old room below:
time to take her to summer school. Five rafters down,
four to go. . .

Biking the hill
we can be quiet. Behind us the new room
blurs in branches and wires. Miranda's eyes
tighten against the wind as she stands on the pedals
and glides, her braids a sudden, brief blond saga.
How did you get to be this old?
                              She rides the last
block alone, seems far away on some shore.
I wave; she laughs, "See you later!" and
disappears.
          Year after year, sun after sun
rolling out the roof— Miranda's childhood
repairs mine, mine covers my father's as his
roofed over his father's. . . Am I amazed for her
or me?
      So what? Love and work, the ache
uphill, up the ladder, onto the roof! Give me
a fistful of 16's and my hammer, this crazyman
above me, and together we'll beat
the last half-sister-of-a-son-of-a-bitch of a rafter
into its rightful place!
                        Three walls.
Three windows. Therefore we have set
2 x 12's on two foot centers
to hold a roof of blue flames.

SOMETHING ICARUS REMEMBERED

My father's garnet ring probably no longer exists—
and could any more than five people now alive
even recall its facet, the window let in through
the nicked gold band so that when light
struck the stone it shone for luck
on the third finger of the wearer?
                          That, anyway,
is why I pinched it from his dresser, luck
which I needed for the season. 40 at-bats
and I was hitless. 216 innings of humiliation
in right field, the suckertrap for the big boys'
bats: They would, as the pitch came,
shift the back foot and plow to right
where everyone knew the gag— my honorary
.300 average for all the balls
I dropped.
            Something, not God, I needed
against myself; I put on the garnet ring.
All the way across town I worked on my hand,
hypnotizing it like a chicken head,
teaching it to Hit and Catch,
Hit and Catch. . .
                    The first ball that came calling,
the charm crushed my finger bones, and the second time
I was shimmying the ring off,
glove between my legs, and the third time
I was trying to remember where did I put
that darned ring, toeing the grass,
looking for it, mumbling our mantra,
No batter no batter no badder no badder,
already the concoction for Dad
brewed outside the foul lines of truth.
And the fourth or fifth time I looked up
I understood the judgement of garnet:
Our inning in life might never end nor would
practice make us perfect.

And still I am looking up:
the ball in its warhead arc hones in, the sun
signs the windows on Church Street with
a bloody scythe, the widow in her boarding room
laughs at this boys' life, and I stand there, salt,
His Eternal Distance chalked out for my understanding
of right field. . . My heart croaked in its
coagulated pond, leapt, too late, for the fly—
Sputnik dropped like a dexedrine and I must catch it
catch it kid catch it! The coach threw his cap
in the dirt, the tanks trampled Manhattan,
the other team polkaed, the warts of Nikita Khruschev
mooned me from the shore. I sweat so much
the cup of my jock set sail with the traitor on board,
I confessed, the cyanide sizzled my lips
but the coward spit it out, the pill blew red
and eight furies screamed Mineminemine!
Later
I broke into the Presbyterian cemetary and hid
in one of the chancels of wealthy death.
Later I would forget about the League and the Ring.
Later there was going to be age and privilege
and the funny rubber pills on garter belts;
and whereas the stockings of that moment were
a moth-bitten torment, the hosiery of my rebirth
would be like the outlaws' trail into fragrant sage,
knowing Miss Moonlight's wink.
I was too tired and numb
that night to cry or pound the marble of the innocent crypt.
I untied my shoes and tapped the dirt from the cleats.
I pulled off those underworld blue legs
and my soaked white socks and all I could think to do
was rub my feet until if not the ache, at least
all hope left them. Sweetie, at that moment

our separate lives began their first unfettered steps
towards each other. We became not more substantial,
but tenuous, vestal as we moved into
the wounded world with its ice-green floor
and its vault of varicose starlight above our
night-colored curls. Would I have seen you then
in the dim reflection when I picked up my socks
to leave, would I have known your face above my own?

That evening, though the ball eluded me,
I had fielded the skin of sky, or began to, for
I have been sloughing it into poems as the sky
gives it down. I do not know where
the ring went, or the boy, or the sky.
I know there is in us the scar of the past entire,
which only love, or luck, slackens and eases away,
whimsical. The old donkey moon is only
a cleat mark in sand, the starlight pours
satin pajamas on those who see, and now
when I hold your hands as I hold no others,
I let go below us something Icarus remembered:
some sheer hose for the newly doomed boys
while together we pull each other through ourselves.
No one has ever heard of us. The light
shines through like someone else's days.

THIS PLACE BY SYCAMORE CREEK

Oh it all starts up on the hills, where the biggest
cow I've ever seen moos the encouragement
of milk, amazing the grasses and me.
Sunlight at this time of day gives way gracefully
to the lesser lights of land— the pure yellow
of poppies; blood-red mallow; and primrose whiter than
your first tooth! Some flowers are so small
you have to praise them from your knees. And, like that,
they open, sky-lights of earth, the heart's flags blazing.
Why even my pee enlightens: soda bottles,
garbage-kissing bees, tourists on their way. . .
Dear Madam in your Oldsmobile, forgive me but
I have to run, I can't stay still!

These two are jojobas, the cowboy's coffee, mated like swans.
Here's acacia; and Santa Rita, Burbank, beavertail.
Greasewood and sage, and lots of buckhorn— I know
they don't need me to tell them, but what pleasure,
to speak with no other purpose! The first time
I stopped here, with Nick, the generator wouldn't charge—
we pulled over to have a look. Unbolted it, popped
the brushes: It was them alright, worn thinner
than dirty fingernails. Nick was an incredible mechanic!
With popsicle sticks he wedged the brushes
against the stator. We finished; passed an old t-shirt
back and forth to wipe our hands; and, seeing
where we'd come, stood a long time in moonlight.
In Oraibi later that week I got sick. Nick drove me home
in four hours! Last I heard he'd gone to Israel.
Another time I was making snowballs when I found
a fine hunk of red jasper. I still have it,
home in the fish-tank. And down on the creek
where a cottonwood had fallen, all afternoon, once,
I whittled weird beasts into the roots.

This place by Sycamore Creek is not just a roadside
stop of the mind. It takes time for a history of love!
You have to dilly-dally along, indulging the little
plants you step on, begging your own forgiveness, because

the past isn't true, and it isn't a lie. Simply,
it happened. We left our memory as a land
outside us, devising our loveliness
so what we lost as form, we return to in love, again.
Yes, it's the time of day when earth is heaven,
and to be on these hills, near a road, by a river,
is the only real chance. Around me here is every one
and thing I've ever loved— even you! Oh, maybe you don't
believe it; but you're here anyhow, with all the beauty
your losses have come to, because for you, too,
the road leads to and from the symmetry of home.
Memory of ourselves— these stories we become of love—
enheartens the earth with our desire to be seen.
These flowers like to be flowers again, joyful and plain!
I'm picking the no-names, violet ones and yellow, this
pretty thing with the faint inner star!
Fragrances and colors, the delicate deliverance of touch,
transform us beyond remembrance. Perhaps this moment
will not go on and I'll wake up in a pumpkin by the road.
It doesn't matter. All I started to say is,
thank you! I'm grateful I can love my life.
Now, right now, I'm happy, I'm happy, I'm so happy!

THE SMALL MOUNTAINS

Now I get up from nailing floor boards
onto the joists, rubbing the ache
that swells my knees and wrecks my mind.
Rusted clamps. Twisted pine. Thumb blooming
a rose of blood— I've forgotten the reason
I started. Here: my bleached frame walls,
plastered with thin air. There: pure distance,
finished without a trowel.

For nine days I have envied the far away,
the small mountains no bigger than seeds,
the mountains I believe in because they can't
be seen! Who knows how long they've been there,
or where among them nest the cooing birds of youth?
Hello, hills. Welcome to our land!
This is the house
I dedicate to you, a space in air where
you can root in the nail-holes I have set.
Here are the springs where mountains can dine,
the oasis where you will kneel. My yearning
will be your sign: Someone remembered. Someone
knew that you would come, drifting and dreaming
into shape. What a journey our life is,
to help the vague take hold! Someone understood—
now the mountains will thrive.

Maybe they'll just guffaw: Who the hell was this?
Who made this mess? Who kissed so much?
Who gushed goodbyes? Who worked here,
whistled and groaned? And why,
when the Great Heart beats in his head,
when he gets up to greet it, why is it gone;
and this ghost, this guest, this friend
stares now at bare boards, hurt by beauty,
by beauty forgiven, each time he kneels again
to hammer.

VIVALDI IN NEW SHOES

If I hadn't looked into the trash can
everything would have been the same. Who
threw out my wonderful old shoes, who
forsook my rights? Who took the well-oiled
machine I am and dumped vegetables and stove-
grease all over it just when the foot was
becoming the wheel? I had to endure the pomade
of salesmen, their cheerful balm— I was not
made for this! Yesterday, in my vulnerable hour,
I sold out to fancy track shoes, even though
I hate running and they came just in gray. But
in those shoes—
oh I was possessed! New feet!
Twin princesses I could hardly believe were mine!
Goodbye ugliness! Goodbye complaints! Take all
my money! This feeling is worth it!
What did I
know about today, jumping around the store
and over my knees, in the magic shoes? Today
at six in the morning I flitted across the hill
trying out for innocence, too close to the sun
in Gemini to turn back to the gawky, lower phyla
with their snot-blowing ox, their hoof-headed ram,
their miracle fish who each year dies
spawning more of my karma.
I was half-way
through my walk. I was talking to an acacia bush,
offering my entire nose to the furry meteorites,
wondering if they could make it into a sachet.
I was fooling around with my shadow which was
either the char left from lightning
or the long back of the blue devil Neptune,
Ruler of Feet. I was turning the walk
into the comedy *Othello* should have been,
about to become Noel Coward and cash in
on my demiurges, when
my questions hit me
with their one-two punch— Who found it necessary

to bludgeon the small rattlesnake into the curve
in the road? Who left it for me
to finish off its writhing and then have to
bend down and massage its wounded side
and marvel at the pale rattle, and first
with a stick, then my actual finger,
trace the clenched jaw where a little blood came,
touching it as I once touched the mouth
of someone I loved while she slept, I did not
want to wake her but now I wish I had
kissed her more, but then I had had enough,
it was time to sleep, I am not a glutton,
nor a ghoul,
             I left it just as I found it
with a smudge of snake blood on my index finger,
and with my questions questions entered the sign
of Neurosis, stalking the cool shade.
In my new shoes, behind my old dog,
I passed through a congregation of finches,
pretending it was a cloud and I Vivaldi
composing a nimbus of yellow palo verde blossoms,
which are almost gone now, which lie like
sun-stains all over the ground. Did I hear
mandolins and harps? Did I hear the vibratto
of heavenly wings scrape the hills again,
chiding us to hurry?

FOR FRIENDS

The bluest evening drifts easily over hills,
seeping from the ground like dye
from the work-shirt, darkening the water.
And this blue! Such a blue it surely cannot last,
shimmering streams, currents of it,
an aura of the about-to-be, like a woman's hair,
falling ahead of her into sleep. . .

The passing of day into night,
the passage of the first day into the last.
Faithfulness to this turn of things
has made me love you, almost despite myself.

Across the field of fenced desert the carpenters
are going home. The houses they are building
are dark, and the houses the sun built in canyons,
the blue house of the sky— blue
made from longing to be one thing!

All day the man builds a blue house
for his woman to live in each night,
and each night she finds this blue house—
she's so tired, it's always where she left it,
whose house could it be? She does not know
she has a lover. Her sleep is so wide it has become
a lake inside himself he wonders if
he'll ever cross. One more night. . .
One more story?— He's been to that face
at the bottom of repose but can't stay awake
long enough to know. Her hair takes his breath away
and keeps it till morning again.

What have we made together, friends, but a small
camp where our desire could spend the night?
Now the last day has come, and I am sad
our time together is ended. Today it is
lonely in my body and I am tired of the strange work
to make one thing another, out of one life

another and another— how many others
till the body of love is complete?

I look in your eyes. So much together
we could make the stars our house! Bear, Hunter,
Virgin, Twins. . . Everything we saw
we named ourselves; now the dust
of what we know blows into our tiniest
constellations. How can we possibly see,
we're so small, so small. We say,
Today. This day. But it is some day
in a blue house of the light we cry for.

This blue light. This blue light that took so long
to speak has come forward from the dark again
like the echo inside the thin iron of blackened bells:
Something from the back of our lives comes forward,
it remembered and came back, taking us
by the hand, leading us where we have always been.

BEDTIME: *WIND IN THE WILLOWS*

Who is shining beside my daughter
as she gargles and brushes at the sink?
Brightness of tinsel sipping our light,
that sparkles back upon us a resourceful task:
to remember we are as yet
unborn. This glittering is myself
blind before the world, before I tumbled
blacked-out backwards down the chute,
lumpy coal for Mama's lap, miraculous tadpole
conjoined of stars— fishpond, bless us, please!

With memory God begins; but where
is that beginning, that preface to a face?
Dad's idea was: Press your cheek
against the glass— feel how cold that is?
Look! Look! A falling star! No,
just a boy like you who wouldn't sleep, who
sneaked from bed and fell through the floor
into the Lord's aquarium!

So now I make it up—
something of rain and sun, a bower
to bend above us; but the moment
speeds on while these facsimiles,
ourselves, hold us here with one more
story, tell one more! Tell about the boy
in the pineapples who ate the snake. Tell
about Rat's guns. Well: *The Rat grew very
grave, wicked faces popped out of holes.* . .

In the Wild Woods beneath the covers
we hold hands. She tries to imagine a Mole
who has never seen one; and I try to see
the angel of return shaking
its dented wings— Oh spirit,
what haven't I been before, from sleep
to sleep repeated? Will the world
I waken in tomorrow be any more complete

because I slept tonight, because I told
a story into dim air, an ordinary father
leaning over a book as if it were
a candle? We humans live in language;
it's you who has a world. Then shine tonight
if I call you nothing, if I silver my hand
in repetition, the brambles
and starlight lies I love, the footprinted
snow. I know desire that makes me speak
can make me whole if I believe
what is weightless in my hand, but will you
remember me when I forget? Will you,
stay, spirit, will you be the breath I breathe
to cool her cheek? When I hum or hurry,
hurry, spirit, hurry to us, be my memory,
my freedom, my little blue jar of songs.

Many friends have helped me over the years with the poems in this book: Brenda Hillman, Tony Hoagland, Steve Orlen, Molly Kent, Lance Patigian, Michael Cuddihy, Karen Dahood, Susan North, Allen Jacobson, Joan Van Dyke and Roger Shanley — thank you. Special thanks to Susan Goldberg and Margo Burwell for their vision and enthusiasm.

Rolly Kent

olly Kent grew up in New Jersey and Vermont. He graduated
om Middlebury College, and after moving to Arizona spent
1any years conducting poetry workshops in rural and reservation
ommunities of the Southwest. Since 1980 he has been the director
f the Tucson Public Library's Writers' Project. His poems have
ppeared in many magazines, including *The American Poetry Review*,
he Atlantic, *Ironwood*, *The Nation* and *Poetry*. He is the editor of
wo special collections of poems: *Southside: 21 Poems by Children*
nd *Willa & Marie: Poems from a Nursing Home* (edited with Susan
lorth). His previous collection, *The Wreck in Post Office Canyon*,
as published in 1977.

Spirit, Hurry was designed by Margo Burwell, a painter and designer living in Tucson. Type was set in ITC New Baskerville and Eras by Kris Gustaveson of Andresen Tucson Typographic Service. The book was printed at Arizona Lithographers in Tucson. Text paper is Beckett Writing Text. Sewn and bound by Roswell Bindery of Phoenix. The cover painting is also by Margo Burwell, *Dream 2,* 1983 (60" x 60", acrylic on canvas) and is reproduced with her permission.